SPORTS secrets and SPIRIT STUFF

by Therese Kauchak

★ American Girl™

Published by Pleasant
Company Publications

Questions or comments? Call 1-800-845-0005,
visit our Web site at **americangirl.com**,
or write to Customer Service, American Girl,
8400 Fairway Place, Middleton, WI 53562-0497.

Printed in China

06 07 08 09 10 LEO 10 9 8 7 6 5 4 3 2 1

American Girl™ and its associated logos are trademarks of American Girl, LLC.

Art Direction: Camela Decaire; Production: Kendra Schluter, Mindy Rappe,

Jeannette Bailey, Judith Lary; Illustrations: Tracey Wood

Dr. Caroline Silby is a nationally renowned sports psychologist, author, and faculty member at
American University. She has worked with two Olympic gold medalists, ten Olympians, three
world champions, eleven national champions, and over 50 national competitors.

This book is not intended to replace the advice of or treatment by physicians, psychologists,
or other experts. It should be considered an additional resource only. Questions and
concerns about mental and physical health should always be discussed with a doctor or
other health-care provider. The publisher disclaims liability for any injuries, losses,
or other damages that may result from using the information in this book.

Dear Reader,

Sport Secrets & Spirit Stuff will help you be a better athlete, no matter what sport you play. Inside this book you'll find what you need to **get stronger, think smarter,** and **have a blast!**

You'll also get **answers** and **advice** from a sports expert who helps both Olympic athletes and girls like you become their best.

So run fast! Have fun! **Go play!**

Your friends at American Girl

Contents

power
drills

Sports Secret:
You don't need fancy equipment to become faster and stronger, or to last longer in any sport.

Practice these drills regularly and you will see your skills improve!

Be Faster

Hop to it! This drill can help improve your speed and jumping ability.

The Plus Sign

The Plus Sign can be done on a gym floor or a dry, hard-surfaced driveway or playground. Be sure to jump with both feet at the same time. Practice regularly, and have a friend time you. Record the number of jumps you do each time, and you can watch your speed improve!

If you're doing this inside, mark off a 4-foot-by-4-foot plus sign on the floor using masking tape. If you're outside, draw the plus sign with chalk.

Begin with both feet in square 1. Jump diagonally to 4 and back again. Repeat for 30 seconds. Count how many jumps you can do in that time.

Rest for 30 seconds. Now switch to the other diagonal, jumping from 2 to 3 and back. Repeat for 30 seconds. Count your jumps.

Extra credit: Done with diagonals? Jump forward—from 3 to 1—and back. Then jump sideways—from 3 to 4—and back. Do 30 seconds of each and rest for 30 seconds in between.

In which direction do you jump the fastest? Keep working on your times, and they'll improve.

Last Longer

Grab a jump rope! Here's another secret: exercises that go from slow to fast, called *interval training,* improve your stamina and endurance.

Fast Forward

1. Skip or jog with the rope, one foot landing after the other. Jog 5 steps forward and 5 steps back. Continue for 1 minute.

2. Speed up your jump-rope jog for 15 seconds. Now go to a slow jog for 1 more minute. Repeat for 2 to 4 minutes.

Bunny Hop

1. Start with 1 minute of steady, regular jumping. Use a 2-footed bounce, with both feet landing at the same time.

2. Without stopping, speed up for 15 seconds. Then slow down for 1 more minute. Repeat this sequence for 2 to 4 minutes.

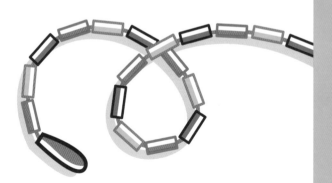

Have Quick Hands

A tennis ball is your secret weapon for becoming better at throwing and catching with both hands.

Popcorn Ball

Play outdoors or in an open gym where there's plenty of room. The key is to keep your eyes on the ball. Watch it all the way into your hand as you catch it.

1. Stand 6 to 7 feet away from a wall. With your right hand, toss a tennis ball overhand at a spot on the wall a few feet above your head. Let the ball bounce back, and catch it with your left hand.

2. Without switching hands, throw the ball again, this time catching it with your right hand. Repeat, continuing to throw and catch with alternating hands.

13

Learn how to send your nerves pack-
ing, stay positive, and talk things out
with parents, boys—even coaches!

Sports Secret:
In sports, brain power is as
important as muscle power!

Handle Your Nerves

Try these tricks to stay relaxed before—and during—the big event.

Hey, Jenny!

BOOOO!

Tune It Out

Athletes who have "rabbit ears" listen too closely to the cheers and to the critics in the crowd. Don't let what other teams—or fans—say get to you. Ignore it and play your game.

What are you doing?

C'mon! Go faster!

Take a Bird's-Eye View

Before the game or match, close your eyes and visualize your performance. Imagine making all the moves you've practiced and see yourself playing your best. It's like watching a highlight film starring you!

Stay Positive

Don't let a onetime mistake seem like a big-time problem. Try these techniques for getting over goof-ups and errors.

Fire the Scorekeeper

Is there a little voice in your head keeping track of everything you do wrong? That's the scorekeeper getting in your way. Fire her! From now on, at the end of a game, congratulate yourself on five specific things you did well.

Close the Drawer

Imagine a tall dresser with many drawers. When you make a mistake, open a drawer, toss in the mistake, and close the drawer tight. You can't see the mistake anymore. It can't affect you, and it definitely won't determine how you'll play in the rest of the game. Lock the drawer and throw away the key.

Are You a Good Sport?

There's no disgrace in losing—it's a natural part of sports. But not every loser is a sore one. What would you do in the following situations?

1. You just lost against a rough opponent. You swear you saw her commit some fouls that the officials missed. You refuse to shake hands with her after the competition.

- **a.** Yes, that's me.
- **b.** I might do this. I shouldn't have to be nice to cheaters!
- **c.** I'd never do this.

2. Your teammate missed a basket at the buzzer that would have won the game. Afterward, you tell her, "It's O.K. Everybody makes mistakes. You're a good player, and this team needs you."

- **a.** I'd never do this. That was an easy shot she missed!
- **b.** I might do this.
- **c.** Yes, that's me.

3. Your team has lost three games in a row. The last game was against a team you thought for sure you'd beat! *If we didn't beat them,* you think, *we're not going to beat anyone. This season will be awful.*

a. Yes, that's me.
b. I might think this.
c. I'd never think this. We may be down, but we're not out.

SCOREBOARD

Sore Loser
If you answered two or more **a**s, you sometimes blame others and dwell on negative thoughts. That doesn't help you! Look ahead to your next game and focus on playing your best.

Crossing the Line
If you answered mostly **b**s, you know in your heart what's right. Focusing on what others did wrong may take away the sting a little, but it isn't O.K. Follow your conscience.

The Winner's Circle
If you answered mostly **c**s, you have the heart of a winner even when you lose. A loss is already history. It's in the past, and there's nothing you can do about it. Keeping a positive attitude will help you start the next game right.

Win Boy Battles

If boys are bugging you on or off the field, try these tips for talking it out.

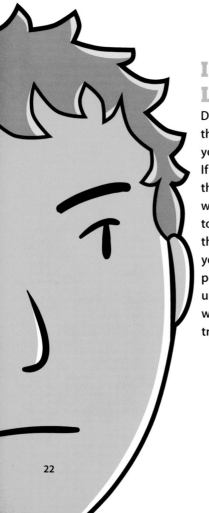

If They Won't Let You Play

Don't accept it. Say to the boys, "Come on, you know that's wrong!" If you can, just join in the game. If they still won't let you play, talk to individual boys from the group afterward. If you can win over a few people, they may stick up for you the next day, when you're back to try again.

Lisa Leslie

Sarah Hughes

Carly Patterson

Cammi Granato

Mia Hamm

Venus Williams

If You Get Teased

If a boy says, "You play like a girl," think of the name of your favorite, most awesome female athlete—you have a ton of choices! Then tell the boy, "I *am* a girl. And so is <u>Mia</u> and she's amazing!"
(her name here)

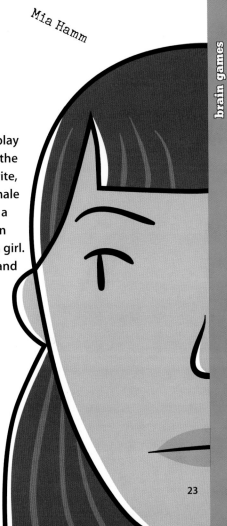

Sasha Cohen

Amanda Beard

Julie Foudy

23

Talk to Your Coach

If you have a problem—say, you feel you don't get enough playing time—don't be afraid to talk to your coach.

Go One-on-One

Talk to the coach yourself instead of asking your teammates or parents to do it for you. Approach the coach when she has time to think about what you're saying, not in the middle of practice. Ask her when she would have time to discuss something important.

Make a Plan

The coach has the final word. If you don't like your coach's answer, ask for help. What can you do to improve? Ask if you could come up with a plan together that would get you where you want to go.

Deal with Your Parents

Most parents mean to be your biggest cheerleaders. Here's what to do when their actions send a different message.

Mr. and Mrs. Loud

Some adults are sure their opinions are the right ones. They argue with officials, criticize coaches, and yell at opposing players.

What to do: If this sounds like your parents, talk to them after the game, when you're both calm. Let them know their actions hurt you. Think of ways to solve a problem when they get upset. If they disagree with the coach, for instance, they could talk to her after the game instead of yelling from the sidelines.

Ma and Pa Pressure

Some adults push their daughter to excel for the wrong reasons—maybe because their other children are sports stars or because they think winning makes them look good. It may feel like these parents are on your back even when the game isn't on your mind.

What to do: If your parents' behavior bothers you, find a quiet time and tell them how you feel. Stay calm and let them know that even though you understand they are trying to help, their words and actions are doing just the opposite—they're hurting.

Put It in Writing

You and your parents can prove that you all understand the meaning of "good sports"—and want to keep things fun—by reading and signing the **Family Sports Promise** on page 63.

Sports Secret:

There's a solution to every problem.

help!

Lots of sporty girls have written American Girl with questions about teammates, coaches, and other sports problems. To get the **best advice,** we went to the big leagues.

Dr. Caroline Silby is a professional *sports psychologist*—a doctor who helps athletes with all aspects of their game, mental as well as physical. She works with Olympic athletes and girls who play all kinds of sports. She has **answers** to all your sports questions!

Q:

DEAR AMERICAN GIRL,

WHEN IT COMES TO SPORTS LIKE
SOFTBALL, VOLLEYBALL, AND EVEN
TENNIS, I STINK! I WANT TO FIND
A SPORT I COULD DO, BUT I GUESS
I'M NOT VERY ATHLETIC.

I'VE TRIED ALMOST EVERYTHING!
NOTHING SEEMS TO SPARK MY INTER-
EST. CAN YOU HELP?

SPORTS STINKER

A:

Here's a new cheer:
> We **think**
> you don't **stink!**

You're doing the right thing by trying different activities. But keep in mind that people's sports skills develop at different times. Even Michael Jordan, one of the greatest basketball players ever, was cut from his high-school team!

You may want to try more recreational activities like bike riding or hiking. Or you could try martial arts, where you can work at your own pace to reach your personal best.

Bonus: Whether you're a superstar or just out for fun, sports teach you more than how to play a game. You learn lessons about friendship, teamwork, goal setting, and effort. Keep at it and be proud of what you achieve!

Q:

Dear American Girl,

I like going to dance class, but I can't stand seeing myself in a leotard. I think I am too big around the middle to wear a leotard, but it's required. What should I do?

Feels Like Dancezilla

A:

Here's another sports secret: chances are, no one else is noticing your looks as much as you are.

It will help if you focus on what you enjoy about dance class rather than on your appearance. Think about what's really important, too—the traits that make you a good dancer, friend, student, daughter, and sister.

Remember that thinness doesn't equal fitness. Try to speak kindly about your body. After all, it's protecting some extremely special gifts—including your happy, dancing feet.

Q:

DEAR AMERICAN GIRL,

I'M WAY TOO SENSITIVE. AT OUR VERY FIRST BASKETBALL PRACTICE, I STARTED CRYING BECAUSE I FELT SO UNCOMFORT- ABLE. CAN YOU HELP ME?

BIG BABY

A:

It's natural to feel nervous in new situations, especially when you want to do well. The key is focusing on something other than your fear, which is what's making you cry. Focus on an action you can control.

Concentrate on your dribbling or on moving your feet quickly. Talk to a teammate, take deep breaths or a sip of water, or move your body from side to side to stay loose.

Learning to tough it out when you're nervous or scared is a skill that will help you in activities for the rest of your life. So, good going—you've already made yourself a better player and stronger girl!

help!

Q:

Dear American Girl,

I have two great friends, and they are both better at sports than I am. They always tell me what I'm doing wrong and then rub it in my face. I think that they think I'm no good. What should I do?

I'm Good, Too!

A:

You need to let your friends know how you feel. Start by telling them you appreciate that they're trying to help you become a better player. Let them know, though, that when they focus on your errors, it doesn't help you. In fact, it discourages you.

Tell your friends that you value their opinions, and that you want to ask for advice when you think you need it. For a while, you may have to remind them that their reviews aren't welcome. You could laugh and say something like, "Too much information!" or "Hello—not motivating!"

Be warm but firm about keeping this boundary with your friends. It will help them to treat you as an equal.

help!

Q:

DEAR AMERICAN GIRL,

EVERY YEAR OUR CLASS HAS TO RUN A MILE. MY BEST FRIEND HATES RUNNING, AND SHE ALWAYS ASKS ME TO WALK THE MILE WITH HER. I FINISH ALMOST LAST WHEN, IF I RAN, I COULD COME IN FIRST!

SHE IS GOING TO ASK ME TO WALK WITH HER AGAIN THIS YEAR. HOW CAN I TELL HER I DON'T WANT TO?

RUNNER AGAINST WALKING

A:

Your friend might not know how you feel. Tell her how excited you are about the run this year! Try explaining that you want to test yourself and see how fast you can be.

Remind your friend that your choice to run has nothing to do with how much you treasure her friendship. Offer to spend some special time with her after the run. Be at the finish line to cheer her on! In the end, this should help your friend respect you for wanting to pick up your pace.

help!

Q:

Dear American Girl,

It seems like only a few people on our team actually try hard. Everyone else just complains about how we lose every game. What can I do?

Tired of Whiners

When the whining is louder than the cheering, there's definitely a problem! It sounds like your team needs someone who leads by example. Why not let that leader be you?

The key is to focus on what the team needs to do to win—then lead the way with your actions. Leave the pep talks and discipline to the coaches. Instead, work hard in practice and praise teammates who work hard. Point out when other girls make good plays. Have a routine that helps you get organized, calm, and focused before the game.

If you consistently focus on the positive, other girls will follow. That should turn the volume on the whining way, way down!

Q:

DEAR AMERICAN GIRL,

THERE'S A REALLY SNOTTY GIRL ON MY SOCCER TEAM, AND SOMETIMES SHE GIVES ME A HARD TIME IN THE LOCKER ROOM. ONCE SHE CAME UP TO ME AND YELLED, "DEODORANT!" LIKE I SMELLED BAD. WHAT SHOULD I DO NEXT TIME SHE HASSLES ME?

LOCKER-ROOM TARGET

A:

This sounds like bullying. If Snotty Girl's comments continue, or if you feel physically threatened, talk to an adult you trust about what's happening.

Meanwhile, remember that bullies enjoy seeing people squirm, so let your personal power shine. Brush off this girl's comments by saying something like, "I worked pretty hard for this smell!" Or sniff your shirt and say, "Smells O.K. to me!"

Stick with other teammates while you're in the locker room. Let your body language send the signal that you're confident. Keep your head up, shoulders back, and chest out. All these steps will let this girl know that you can handle her comments—no matter how snotty they are!

Q:

Dear American Girl,

What should I do if I'm playing against someone and she breaks the rules on purpose—or with the blessing of her coach?

Cheater Spotter

It can be surprising to learn that not everyone plays by the rules! The best thing *you* can do is control your own behavior.

When rules are broken, especially when it happens repeatedly, bring it to the attention of an adult. Start with your coach. State the facts, and avoid preaching and complaining.

Cheaters actually give themselves the biggest punishment of all, because they know that what they are doing is wrong. They end up feeling bad about themselves—which means they lose the most in the end!

Q:

DEAR AMERICAN GIRL,

WHEN I GET CALLED FOR A FOUL, IT'S HARD NOT TO TAKE IT PERSONALLY. WHAT CAN I DO?

GRRRR

A:

If you get called for a foul, it shows you are playing aggressively. That means you play hard and are willing to play your heart out to help the team.

So when the whistle blows, think about your physical contributions to the team—your shooting, dribbling, and passing skills. Then recognize your emotional contributions—your risk taking, hard work, and dedication. Now, those are some *positive* facts you can take personally!

help!

Q:

Dear American Girl,

My dad really likes basketball. Both my brother and I used to play, but he quit. Dad said that was O.K., but he was really crushed.

Now that I play in middle school, I can't stand the competition, the time it takes, and the hard work. I think I want to quit, but I don't want to hurt my dad. Help!

Confused

A:

Let's take a time-out! It's great that you're looking at why you play sports. It may be time to play for reasons other than competing and winning. Maybe you like basketball because you can be around friends, see yourself improve, set and reach goals, or stay in shape.

Quitting altogether may not be the only answer. You could play for a less competitive team, stop competing to work on your skills for a while, take lessons, or try a different sport. Start by having a heart-to-heart with your father about your concerns. He may not know how you really feel.

Q:

DEAR AMERICAN GIRL,

MY LITTLE SISTER AND I ARE IN GYMNASTICS TOGETHER, AND SHE IS BETTER THAN I AM! I FEEL BAD BECAUSE I CAN'T EVEN DO A ONE-HANDED CARTWHEEL.

CARTWHEELER WANNABE

A:

The key to improving is sticking to your goal.

You may take a little longer than others to perfect some of your skills, but remember—gymnastics is not a sprint to the finish line. It's a sport that requires patience and persistence, especially when you're learning tough tricks!

Taking extra time to learn a skill correctly can also help you develop consistency and mental toughness. That's as valuable as learning a one-handed cartwheel!

help!

51

show your
your
spirit!

Play a sport? Show your spirit!
These girls tell you how they keep
team spirits sky-high.

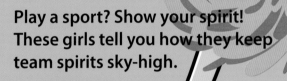

Sports Secret:
Sometimes heart is the
strongest muscle of all.

From Christine

RE: Dress for Success

To show our spirit, my teammates and I wear our jerseys to school on game day. Sometimes we even paint our faces and dye our hair.

From Kelsey

RE: Fluffy Flip-Flops

I cut little strips of fleece in my team colors and tied them around the straps on my flip-flops. I wear them to gymnastics. They're fun and fluffy.

From Shelby

RE: Spirit Scarves

My friend's mom made cool scarves that we wear to practices and meets. She laid 3 pieces of fleece on top of one another and sewed down the middle. Then she made cuts partway into the center to make fringe.

show your spirit!

From Carter

RE: Have Secret Sisters

We do Secret Sisters. Before our first game, we each draw a name out of a bag, and then before every game we secretly give our "sister" a little gift, like healthy food, a sports drink, or a key chain. Before the last game, we tell each other whose sister we were.

From Amanda

RE: Nickname 'em

The girls on my team make up funny—but nice—nicknames to make one another laugh, like "Ally the Alligator," "Bryan the Beast," and "Diane the Dodger."

From Nikki

RE: Pancake Power

On my softball team we had a pancake breakfast at one of the coaches' houses. After the breakfast, all the girls played games together.

show your spirit!

Ten Super Sticker Ideas

Use the mini stickers in this kit to decorate

1. a water bottle for your bike or for workouts.

2. a picture frame. Put in a photo of your team-mates, of you playing your best, or of your favorite lake, park, or ski hill—anyplace you like to play.

3. a school notebook, journal, or team handbook.

4. an I.D. tag for your gym bag or equipment bag. Attach stickers to the back of the identification tag. Make sure your contact information stays clear.

5. a plastic bin to organize small sports equipment or a plastic cup to hold hair supplies. You'll be able to find your goodies when you're about to run outside.

6. small barrettes for holding back your hair while you work up a sweat.

7. a pencil holder for your desk.

8. pencils or pens for inspiration while you write.

9. the handle of a hairbrush.

10. your calendar. Use the stickers to mark days when you are going canoeing or biking, have a game, or are doing something fun.

If you have stickers for a sport you don't play, don't toss them! Use them to decorate a card or stationery for a friend who's a fan of that sport. Or trade stickers with friends.

show your spirit!

Spirit Scrunchie

Use the star ribbon in *Sports Secrets and Spirit Stuff* to make a ponytail holder in your team colors.

1. Have an adult help you cut two pieces of ribbon in your team colors. Each piece should be 17 inches long.

2. Hold the star ribbon between the two other pieces of ribbon.

3. Loop all the ribbons around the scrunchie or ponytail holder, and tie them in a knot. Wear your spirit scrunchie in style!

Star Shoulder Ribbons

Roll the sleeves on a short-sleeved T-shirt and tie them up with pieces of star ribbon. Finish them off with a knot or small bow.

Temporary Tattoos

Show your spirit with a temporary tattoo! See the instructions in the tattoo package inside the *Sports Secrets and Spirit Stuff* kit.

Mini Good-Luck Cards

Big wishes can come in small packages! Use the mini good-luck cards in *Sports Secrets and Spirit Stuff* to send wishes to friends or teammates before a big event. It's especially nice to remember girls who might be nervous. Stick a card in their locker or gym bag!

show your spirit!

Home of the Brave

Every athlete should know the words to the national anthem. Teach them to your friends. Stand up, take off your hat, and sing along!

The Star-Spangled Banner
by Francis Scott Key

O, say, can you see,
by the dawn's early light,
What so proudly we hailed
at the twilight's last gleaming?

Whose broad stripes and bright stars,
through the perilous fight,
O'er the ramparts we watched
were so gallantly streaming?

And the rocket's red glare,
the bombs bursting in air,
Gave proof through the night
that our flag was still there.

O, say, does that star-spangled banner yet wave
O'er the land of the free
and the home of the brave?

The Family Sports Promise

I, _____ ,
(your name here)
promise to do my best in whatever sport I play.

I vow to:

go to practice
play fair
work hard
keep track of my schedule
put away my equipment
and, most of all, always **HAVE FUN!**

_____
(your signature)

I, _____ ,
(adult's name)
promise to support my sporty girl in ways that
will help her shine and grow.

I vow to:

encourage more than I criticize
show respect to coaches and referees
not coach from the sidelines
pay attention during games, even when she's
   not playing
cheer on her teammates, too
not review her performance on the ride home
and, most of all, always **HAVE FUN!**

_____
(adult's signature)

Here are some other American Girl books you might like:

❑ I read it.

❑ I read it.

❑ I read it.

❑ I read it.

is the
**strongest
muscle**
of all.